Bosque

bosque

poems

Michelle Otero

UNIVERSITY OF NEW MEXICO PRESS
CITY OF ALBUQUERQUE DEPARTMENT OF CULTURAL SERVICES
ALBUQUERQUE

Library of Congress Cataloging-in-Publication Data
Names: Otero, Michelle, author.
Title: Bosque: poems / Michelle Otero.
Other titles: Albuquerque poet laureate series.
Description: Albuquerque: University of New Mexico Press,
    City of Albuquerque Department of Cultural Services, 2021. |
    Series: The Albuquerque poet laureate series
Identifiers: LCCN 2020040385 (print) | LCCN 2020040386 (e-book) |
    ISBN 9780826362698 (paperback) | ISBN 9780826362704 (e-book)
Subjects: LCGFT: Poetry.
Classification: LCC PS3615.T476 B67 2021 (print) | LCC PS3615.T476 (e-book)
    | DDC 811/.6—dc23
LC record available at https://lccn.loc.gov/2020040385
LC e-book record available at https://lccn.loc.gov/2020040386

Cover photograph courtesy of Steven St. John
Author photograph courtesy of Henry Rael
Designed by Felicia Cedillos
Composed in Adobe Caslon Pro 11/14

ONE
ALBUQUE
RQUE
cultural services

Published in association with the City of Albuquerque
Department of Cultural Services

for 'Burque
y para Nuevo México,
estas tierras encantadas que amo con todo mi ser

Contents

The Color Brown

coyote fence   backyard dirt   January yucca frond   Estancia pintos
arroyo sand   sun-cracked gourd   cottonwood trunk   husk
dust   mesquite pod   dirt road   river clay   adobe brick
Taos church   mother's hands   me

Aquí Estamos

We are older than this country, created
in the collision of peoples from across oceans
and the center of the earth.

We come from people who work, people
who dream. We are scholars and writers,
científicos y senadoras.

We come from people who serve
in every war
in every capacity.

We come from loss,
de lucha y logro.

Somos de abundancia, de *donde*
come uno, comen dos. We come from
the table leaf, the TV tray, Grandpa's workbench,
lo que sea para acomodar más.

We come from ghosts, de recuerdos
de la casa de Nana y
las manos de Abuelo.

Somos de chile colorado
de metate y molcajete
de cumbia, flamenco, tango y
cha-cha-cha.

We are morenas with blue-black hair
güeros with green eyes
threads of morado under the skin.

Somos lodo y álamo

We are corn
We are rock

We are willow and reed
dust and ash

We drink river
burn cedar
make mountain
make rain

Sabemos
Somos sabios,
sanadoras y milagros

They say hearing is the last sense
to leave the dying.
So what is it we need to say?

The ombligo will always lead you home

We know each other
Let us remember
the speck in your eye makes
my eye water

I see you because I
see myself, hear you
because I know the sound of my own voice

Let us remember ourselves whole
Let us re-member
we are corn, bean, and squash

May we plant truth
harvest transformation
May we relearn this language
we've always known
lenguaje más allá de la lengua
lenguaje del río y del corazón
de tierra, del alma y del sol

A Prayer of Thanks for the Givers

you give to remember the words de esa canción de cuna que te cantaba Amá
you give to practice the steps Daddy taught with your feet on top of his
you give to learn what our books missed
you give to make home

you make bricks on the plaza
school buses in the lot
altares a los muertos
divas and dance—folklorico, flamenco, salsa, and ballet
creas pintura y poesía, teatro y tertulias
you make arepas, sancocho, pupusas, y flan

you give to remember red chile in a butter container, geraniums in a coffee can
you give because Abuelo fought in World War Two,
because your mom always wanted to be in a play
you give because that guitar under the bed won't let you sleep at night
you give to learn what our parents missed
no por su culpa—por miedo, por vida, para protegernos

creas cuentos y colchas
marchas y matachines
you give gritos and carnaval
resolanas y raspados

you give because *Última* was the first book you read that told your story
because you grew up in a house on Mango Street

you make beauty
you make seeds, make roots

you give because la cultura cura
because this is home

you give to come home
to make a new home
familiar and ever changing
a home that makes the world bigger and smaller at the same time

you give who you are
and it makes us who we are

gracias
y gracias

Water

We tell the children tales
of thunderstorms. Each May we drop
rose petals into trickling acequia, invoke
San Ysidro for good harvest, good rain
pray these petals seed clouds. We remember
summers of fire, haze over mesa, sunset behind a scrim
of smoke, torches in the Jemez, torches in the Sangres
kindling night roads from Santa Fe to Santo Domingo.

What if it never rains again?

What if
      it never rains
                  again?

Pillar of Seed

we, cast kernel
or seed wing feathered
to soil   black or red or nest

we, seed relations, speak
seed language, craft root
letter, whip tendril tongue,
click-clack fava bean teeth

we, dryland parable
vocation   we, heirloom
nothing common about us   at all

Tierra Encantada

Show me
Scarlet runner
Apple sapling
Flea-beetle bite

Show me
Red corn nest
Lanceleaf sage
Garlic scape

Show me
Paper husk
Mud cloud
Soap root

Dandelion, show me to use the whole of you

Show me
Horsetail
Crow
Hand holding stick

Show me milpa
Chicomecoatl glass gem
Altar

I offer my hands

Seed Packet for Dry Land

Wrap in old rags
Plant after last freeze
shoulder-deep in dark soil

Drop water to survive dry times

      how to measure sunlight
      how to thrive when late
      rain, no rain, elk raid, frost

You know this

      everything breaks
      to become what it is
      you know this

It is all dry land

When time comes winnow
Grind into coarse flour   Take
to river where

we are enough

Rain

We remember Isleta Feast Day.
Hide drum.
Dancers pray with their feet.
One chin, then another
turns to sky.
Two gold eagles circle,
conjuring clouds.
One drop, then another.
Stillness, except
the drum
the dance
the rain.

Sunday morning we cross
Central Bridge on foot, called
by the same spirit drawing
     hiking boots
     cowboy hats
     hard-creased Dickies
     running shorts
     pigtails
     plastic rosary hanging from a walker
     nose rings
     Oakland Raiders tattoos

We stand in silence on the banks of the Río Grande, pilgrims
no less awestruck than John the Baptist's converts
for the miracle of a river at its highest point in forty years.

For a moment
we forget
our thirst.

Bosque Walk, Groundhog Day

Olive tree feeds Cedar Waxwing.
Groundhog sees early spring.
Sixty degrees in February.

In photograph nephew holds utility knife.
In Facebook post he asks, *neck or wrist?*

I look at everything
like it's going to die.

How much longer, Waxwing? Groundhog? Nephew, how
much longer?
　　　Do you think you're the only one?
How much longer, olive, bosque, woman wearing
my skin these forty-eight years?

Bosque, like poetry, says *pay attention.* Woodpecker
taps a trunk. Pill bug turns leaf
to lace.

Tierra

Land of plenty?

        Donde come uno

Land of

        comen dos.

enough.

In Praise of Pods

—*after Pablo Neruda*

Late summer I sleep in a red chile pod
on a tin roof in Tomé
Perseids storm above us
showering seeds.

I shape stem and calyx into a hat that whispers
when to plant,
how to weather drought,
the tortilla recipe Grandma never wrote down.

Mornings I sweep seeds into a pod purse
to store in sótano until spring.
Praise you, pods, celestial beings,
constellation come home.

Praise the serrated knife in Mother's hand
slicing crown, severing placenta
scattering seed into brown paper bag.
Praise the lilt of you soaked in water

softening for blender blade. Praise
the blender, Mother's ears attuned
to the whir, slowing as chile thickens.
Praise the knowing.

More pods.
Now garlic.
Water here, salt there.
Flour—never.

Praise the white shirt tempting
as canvas to oils. Praise your capsaicin
sting in the mouths of 'manitos
desde Mora hasta Mimbres.

Praise the pods that make our homes.
Nana's red-stained Tupperware, neighbor
tending rows after his wife died.
Our trade—his chile for our corn.

Precious harvest drying on tin roofs
you grace the table of every meal
ladled over egg, scooped into tortilla,
better than butter on bolillo.

You are pool for pork and flakes flaming
chocolatl, drink of gods. Vaina que da
vainas entre familiares y extranjeros
nos hace familia, todos.

Pods, que sigamos soñando
bañados en metéoros
contentos con la calentura
de techos de tina.

Because the Kitchen

We have a place to stand
at parties, pick that last
chicharrón off the paper towel,
dip a tortilla into red chile
como bendición.

We have a place to gather
when Abuela dies.
Menudo simmering on the stove.
Bolillos warm in a kitchen towel.
Three mismatched bowls—lime wedges, oregano, chopped onion.
Shots of Jack Daniels around the table.
(She always kept a bottle under the sink.)
Mom and her sisters laugh at their mama's
tough love because they aren't ready
to cry.

I know what to do when babygirl holds
her tummy, pink blood in the toilet. Walk her
back to bed, heat a sock of rice
in the microwave, prepare a cup of manzanilla.
We'll be late to fifth grade today. Sometimes
the body grows before we are ready.

Tía stirs instant coffee while
Grandpa reads the obituaries.
Dad works a crossword before sunrise,
leaves for work while the house sleeps,
while the kitchen fills with light.

My first rolling pin was an empty Tecate bottle
I baked bread and bread was love
I hand-fed the stray who made me his home.

We dim lights, sing Las Mañanitas
from Rey David to San Pedro.

Sometimes miracles happen.

Sometimes we hide
only to find ourselves.

In this kitchen
we make light
we make lives
we make sisters—three and three and three again until
we make family until
we make ourselves whole
and whole again.

How to Write about Service

Remember the grandmothers, tortillas
inside a kitchen towel on a floured countertop.
Stove always giving. They were the first volunteers.
They taught you that food is love is family is waking
before light so coffee comes up with sun, taught
you to speak fried onion, comino, tripe. Filled
you up until you had enough to give.

To write about service remember the grandfathers—
mechanics, veterans, they worked their hands, taught
you to play baseball, choke up on the bat, always
go down swinging. They were tender men. We knew
them after the stories formed; the things that didn't
kill them made us stronger.

Remember Mother. She taught elementary school
for thirty years. She said, *you're special* and
we're no better than anybody else.

Remember Father, who sold your Girl Scout cookies
to his coworkers at the plant, told you to write *laborer*
under parent's occupation on all those college forms.

Remember the neighbor, that person Jesus
told us to love.

Remember Isabel. She lived across from you. Picked
up an extra box of popsicles or a bag of oranges
from the Price Rite because they were on sale
and the kids might like them.

Remember Alan, friend of a friend
of a friend. He worked your college
essays until the acceptance letters
came. Sent you to school with a list
of names and numbers of all
the other brown kids in Boston.

Remember why
I serve because I love
I serve because I am
because you are
because we must
because if not us, then who
this place, like God, has no
hands but ours, no feet
but mine and yours
so walk with me. No voice
but ours so shout
we are love
we are 'Burque
we are one
we are 'Burque
we are love
we are 'Burque
we are one

Water

Here water
gives   water takes.   Paraje   Los Árboles   San Rafael   flooded, burned,
buried
for reservoirs and dams.

Water controlled.
Water contained.

Salt cedar, Siberian elm, Russian olive stem
Río Grande, root
deep
as though
they belong.

Women's Work

—*after "The Spinners, or The Fable of Arachne"*
by Diego Velázquez

Back turned, barefoot, Arachne sits at skein.
Fates feed yarn.   She should have been
humble when the goddess appeared as hag.

        Powerful women
        shape-shift
        to crones. Bite
        the apple. Step inside
        her candy house.

She challenged Athena
weaver to weaver. The goddess revealed
her helmet and sword.

        Powerful men
        show up as they are.
        The devil is always
        the best-looking man
        at the dance.

    When I am too big
    I am the painter's Arachne
    Face turned. Get to work.

Athena, wheel. Arachne, skein.
Athena spins warning—
gods besting men, daughters throwing
themselves to sea. Arachne weaves
testimony—Zeus rapes
Europa, Hades abducts
Persephone.

I keep a python
wrapped around
my left femur. She pulses
when threat
is great. I open
my skin to let
her out.

We know what happens
to Arachne.

The python took up residence
one morning. There's always
a hand grabbing something
it shouldn't. Always a sword—
silence.

Consider the deadliest weave.
Consider Charlotte,
Araneus cavaticus, blowing
her web to save a pig. Consider
my thigh, a threat.

Untitled

What is the cure for sand
in the throat?

Ask the river.

Poetry Walk

My natural surroundings try to leave me alone.
Cicada doesn't need me to be.
I tighten my bootlaces to enter the wilderness

of myself. Bug-sprayed and SPF-slathered, tethered
to traffic stream. I wait for hunger, rub my eyes,
imagine losing a contact lens, and then what

would I see? My husband could be cottonwood
or bear. When I leave the civilization of me
I wait for my hair to tangle in nest,

for dirt to gather in fingernails.
When was I last alone? What
are my landmarks? Sorrow

in belly, chicken pockmark etched in lip. Mother's hunger,
mulberry stripped of bark. Grandpa's fear,
the far bank. Grandma's rage, the path.

Sandbar, a ship inside me, empty garage
where Grandpa fixed cars. Shell casing, gun nest,
child seed never watered. I had a dream

of being a bird. When have I ever
fallen to my knees in gratitude?
Does the ant bend under object?

Does it feel the heaviness?
Natural surroundings, call me.
Tell me my name.

Time

Who will remember our prayers?
Who will harvest the corn?
Who will sweep the graves?

To Grow a Child in New Mexico

You were born a cottonwood spore
In drought

You were born in monsoon

You were born in a season of fire

You were born flor de tuna
Rodeada de espinas

You were born headfirst
In the center of the earth

⁓

You learned to crawl among Mother roots
Learned Mother tongues

You fed on stories and flour tortillas, suckled
Caldo from grandmothers' fingertips

You were raised by many mothers
By atole in a tin cup,
By the light of a south-facing wall

⁓

You forgot your language

The road washed out behind you

You fought a war nobody knows

You came home

You never left

⁓

You were hierba buena

You were hierba del manso

You were passion flower named for Christ

⁓

What does it take to grow a child?
More sunlight, water? Well-
Drained soil?

What if butterflies, guitarra y acordión?
What if bosque? If dicho y hecho? If
Paintbrush, if pluma?

⁓

We pray for you with our hands
Fashion a vessel of mud, of bone

Hearing is the last sense
To leave the body
We work to give you enough
To speak to us
Enough to sing

Ode to the Explorers

Praise explorers of quiet library corners.

Praise the guides—librarian, tutor, interlibrary
loan, database, key clicks—holding distant
collections within adobe, holding lanterns
up to cave walls: see this, see here, see beyond.

Praise the women, bodies of work
that show us who we are. Praise
Galindo, Nakadate, Abramovic, exploring
danger and control across language
and time.

Praise mimesis and diegesis, white teeth
we hone on bone, refine to fine point
and bite, one search, one word,
one paragraph at a time.

Praise the hands stilling sullied cloth, shaken
over landscape and river, the net catching
contaminants as they fall to soil. Praise slow
fashion, textiles tethering us to earth.

Praise the brothel, the tavern, the prison, the inn,
between-space, where shadow sets
and story dwells along the scaffolding
of gender.

Praise *The Death of Socrates*, *Oath
of the Tennis Court*, enlightened work,
each brushstroke steeped in the history
of France. Praise the artist colorful
as the canvas.

Praise CRISPR, the poetry
of endocytotic fate, mesoporous
silica nanoparticle, the lipid
bilayer. Praise the roots
of healing in university labs.

Praise the Hulsmans, Mary Lois and Jim, keepers
of fire and wisdom. Your gift lives
in young scholars' words, sparking
flames for generations to come.

Ode to the Art-Makers

Praise the Bravos. Después de tres años
de descanso, your curtain rises again.
We missed you. May you open more doors,
shatter more ceilings with roses tossed
at your feet.

¡Bravo!
Well done.
Congratulations.
Splendid.

Praise Montgomery! Your art is action. You are poet and clown,
sculptor and singer, dancer and scholar. Your art is a gateway
to ourselves—looking inward and outward, behind and before us.

Praise Sarita—mujercita, burqueñita
hija del sol y mucho más. Vuela mariposa,
desde la hoja hacia el infinito.

Praise Zavier! You are woke, hyped up, hip-
hop, lit. You speak music. You are light,
and where you go, everyone shines.

Praise Maggie! Your life is art. Your work
is the heart—ever growing, brushstroke
by brushstroke, story by story.

Praise Kei & Molly! Entire continents reside in your prints.
Journeys across oceans and wars, famine and drought
turn to dance on your factory floor. The work of your hands
holds the bread, holds tortillas, wipes the counters, adorns altares.
Bluebonnets and bees, piñatas and pomegranates, cranes, books,
bugs, and sage. You make home wherever you go.

Praise Ebony, honeysuckle creative, grinning, bare.
You make medicine—soothing souls, easing breath.
Filling teacups with bosque flower, seed, and leaf.
You sing moon, sing sun, sing Black women's bodies, spit
story, spit rhyme. You make auntie, make mother, make hermana,
make friend, make makers, make space, make noir.

Praise Lee Francis, Native Realities. No, really.
For real Red Planet. For real Indigenous Comic Con.
In your hands, culture is here is now is future
as you line bookshelves of Indiginerds with
Tales of the Mighty Code Talkers, Tribal Force,
The Wool of Jonesy. Yours is not culture preserved,
but culture alive, elevated, reflecting reality, seeding
resistance.

Circo, te festejamos. Under your tent
children find balance on one wheel,
a tightrope, six-foot stilts. You are steady
and ever changing, a summer home
for gente. Under your wings
children soar.

Praise Ideum, your workshop no less magical
than that of Santa's elves. In your installations
an invitation for every child in every museum,
Yes! Touch this! Praise the lights
against our fingertips, the designs of ancients
made life-size. You might exist anywhere,
but you could only live here.

Praise Pilar and Frank! You conjure Orishas,
drums and the balls of your feet baptized in the Caribbean.
You are calypso y carnaval, movimiento y maestros.
White skirts and steel drums, your legacy is joy.

Praise the creatives, makers of rhyme
crafters of heroes, chroniclers of time.
Praise the Indiginerds, the honeysuckle,
lavender towels, stilts and samba.
Praise silhouettes and slam,
Right Reflection and Flight.

Congratulations
Splendid.
Well done.
¡Brava!

Ode to the Makers

Praise the makers
the givers of art
the storytellers
and dancers, space-holders
and scene shapers. Praise
the hands that adorn us,
makers of beauty and soul.

Praise the jewelers
you melt us down to our essence
strip all that is unnecessary
find the ore, a vein of gold—
a bench, a teacher, a torch and hammer.
Bravo Meltdown, in your space there are no metals
too small, no wax so lost it can't be cast.

Praise Rujeko, brave dancer, kick, arms wide open. Inhale.
Exhale. The road you have chosen travels
out and back to you. You make dancers, make story
for and from women, make rain. You stretch dance,
make it bigger than we know, as big as we can be
and beyond.

Alabanza, John Acosta, in your hands
a camera is lifeline to brown boys and men.
In your hands, South Valley is place, is home
con bancos de cempasúchil. You reel our diary,
show us who we are. Your hands
grant peace to all our raza.

Praise the Circus! In your rings all are welcome.
In your rings, we heal through art and story,
through light and song.

Bravo, Trupthi. Your dance is more than steps.
Your dance is water, is poem, is spark. Your dance
is people, is story, is map and language and
tongue to speak.

Praise Off Center, your birds of play,
your open door is permission to paint, to make,
to create and cocreate. *Can I make this?* Yes. *Can I
take it home?* Yes. Through your open door
we are centered.

Alabanza Amanda, you are power, engine to writers
and lovers of words. Reader and writer
of fine print, pathway to the press. You ask,
How can I help? And answer in presence and
word.

Viva Revolutions. You show us art lives here—
far from coasts, in 'Burque streets and
black boxes. Art to art, creator to creator,
you make magic from the mundane,
lift us up to stage light, make us shine.

Sheri Crider, bearer of light. The creator,
the Kestrel, the Wheatear alight in your company,
take flight at the crossroads of experience, equity
and empathy. You restore humanity, return us
to ourselves. In your company, we belong.

Praise Frank, el padrino, your legacy of landscape and musical line.
Esta tierra encantada corre por tus venas
y sale de tus dedos hacia la tela, hacia la guitarra
hasta el corazón del 'manito. Nos vemos
en tu cuadro, nos escuchamos en tu canto.

Praise the artists, the hands that hold us,
those who re-member
and give us back to ourselves
sin tí, no seríamos nosotros.

Language

They didn't
teach us Spanish.
Didn't want us
punished in school,
our names
changed. Didn't
want us to sound
Mexican.

Where the Border Isn't a Metaphor

A poet on my Borderlands panel
says when he was a boy he thought the lines
dividing countries were real, thought he could
touch them if he crossed one side to the next.
I think of my older brother who, as kids, told me
the stars pinning capital cities to maps
were visible from airplanes. That's how they know
where to land. He said the lines between states
were dotted so we could drive across them.
The lines between countries were solid. We needed
permission to cross. That's why there were guards.
From the kitchen, my mom, lesson plans and first-
grade writing sheets fanned around her, called out,
Stop telling her those things! She believes you.
We were born north of that line dividing
New Mexico from her older sister, the one who just
couldn't get it together, where Customs asked
each time we crossed back from the dentist, the Pink Store,
the eye doctor, the pharmacy for penicillin without
a prescription, *US citizens?* On the Borderlands
panel the poet invites me to enter the borderless realm
of my imagination. I recall junior year when our Wild-
cat marching band paraded the main road of Palomas.
I played a trumpet solo, "America the Beautiful," while
school kids in green uniforms waved Mexican
and American flags. The governors of Chihuahua
and New Mexico shook hands to launch a surveillance blimp
to help the Border Patrol catch drug runners and smugglers
and people who looked like us. We were served
lunch in a dance hall with high ceilings and dusty
light from open barn doors. We ate carne asada and drank

Coca-Cola from bottles. I said *gracias* when a girl my age
picked up my empty plate, my only Spanish.
My parents didn't teach us, didn't want anyone
mistaking us for Mexicans. There have always been walls.
Consider the bobcat, Chihuahuan desert split in half. Ask
my brother and me. In English so we understand.

Dwelling

We built from rust-colored stones stacked
atop one another, terrón blocks of river clay,
Spruce-fir fences, mud-oven mounds, made
homes to crumble back to earth.

You Make the Library Friend

You make the library Río Grande
swollen in monsoon, young
willow rooting deep, finding home.

You make the library bosque—
morning mist rising with crane,
woodpecker, waxwing.

You make the library Abuela's kitchen,
where there's always strong coffee,
a seat at the table, and stories of who we are.

In your hands library is mud-
mortared terrón block house,
cool in summer, sturdy, safe.

Library is front-porch guitar,
percussion hands, song
we know by heart.

In your care, library is medicine
filling small hands with books
to keep.

With you library is pueblo,
the people, where we come
to know ourselves.

Breaking Ground

Caravan East sign says, *Breathe
in this moment.* We break
ground in this place where we
cumbia'd to Al Hurricane,
two-stepped to Glen Campbell. *Breathe in*

this moment, when we stand together
by standing apart, holding our touch
for another time. We break ground
in this place of ghosts, strong souls
spiriting us across oceans, whispering

stories in wind. This ground
of sawdust-covered floors. This ground—
alluvial plain off Sandias, where roots
of corn, bean, squash compact under asphalt, converge
on Route 66—journey's beginning or end
or just passing through. We break ground

to say, *Stay with me. Sit. Tell your story.*
Journeys across states, over continents,
through cloud and ocean se encuentran
aquí en la mesa made of books. We breathe
in this moment, break ground,

break bread—
phô and fufu, fry bread, fideo
ashak and arroz con pollo.
In this moment, we stand together
by standing apart. My mask is

your shield. Your mask is mine.
It won't always be this way.
We break ground to grow
something new, build from seeds
planted before we were born.

We water shoots pushing
through concrete. We are all colors
of sunrise over Sandias, welcoming
us home.

Little House 4 Sale

A particleboard sign leans against the Tuff Shed
Johnny flipped to a loft,
letters spray-painted red
>Little House
>4 Sale
>$7000

This is home, inside the bent elbow of a road
without sidewalks, the remains of land
divided and subdivided. March through
October the acequia runs behind him,
his dad's house next door, close enough to hit
with butts flicked off his porch.

One afternoon the cleanest white
truck Johnny ever saw pulled
up and parked, so close he could touch
the grill from where he sat on a kitchen chair
on his concrete stoop. He smoked American Legends
while a woman ran an electric
razor over his neck hairs.
>¿Y esa mujer? Skin the color of Crown Royal poured into tight jeans,
>she walks the road with no sidewalks to Casa Liquors, the corner
>store, the tire shops on Bridge. Her hips sway like a cobra under
>a charmer's spell, her hips the cobra and the spell.

He had never seen the driver but could tell
he was all official y todo
from the logo on the door, the words
Bernalillo County, State of New Mexico
made a circle around a blue sky
that matched the vato's button shirt. A zia sun

warmed white sheep on a green field
              or maybe they're cows?
in two lines like they're marching to a matanza
              why don't they eat the grass?
The vato closed the truck door,
pulled a tape measure off his belt. Johnny asked,
Hey bro, you gonna put us some sidewalks?

By the time the truck pulled away,
Johnny had six months to move. Turns out
he's squatting on county land. To think
they never would have noticed, if
his dad hadn't pitched a roof
              without a permit
on his cinderblock casita, blocking the neighbors'
mountain view, neighbors from the street with green
grass and coyote fences, nice people who retire in a
fixer-upper that a from-here family can't afford
to keep
              or maybe they could, but why when
              you get more house on the west side
              and it's new?
Those neighbors spent
a year battling permits and zoning
just to build a higher fence separating their acre
from the likes of Johnny and his shed.

On land that isn't really his, he turned
a clothesline post into a chin-up bar,
made a fence of elm trunks the Army Corps
tagged orange for removal from the bosque
              they didn't mean removal by him.

Warm afternoons he sits on the trunk, waves
at passing cars, flags down La Cobra for a cigarette
                    or smack or some
                    other favorcito.

He wears track pants and chanclas
with worn heels. He wears loose tank tops
that hang over his belly. He wears
a rhinestone cross on a gold chain.
Johnny, a close-cut fade,
as much gray as black now,
his face always shiny. He's
not bad-looking. Not really. Dark
eyes, full cheeks and lips,
the scab in his brow hardening,
like mud he could wash
with spit and his finger. Not
fat, no pués. . . . He should
eat better. He should stop
smoking. He should take
the meds they gave him
at the clinic.

He hasn't held a job since
Social Security declared him disabled,
his body strong, but the mind
flies in strange directions. He forgets
which pill to take when. He shouldn't drink.
He fills prescriptions with what's flowing
at the confluence of acequia and pavement,
miniatures from Casa Liquors, spice at
the head shop on Bridge and La Vega, and chiva
delivered to your door.

For a season he harvests rainbow
chard, yellow pear tomatoes and golden
beets at a neighbor's farm. His boss grew

up on the same ditch, wears diamond-
stud earrings, a barbed-wire tattoo on
his bicep. The farm is a backyard and
fallow fields turned a generation ago
from beans and chile to alfalfa and sorghum
                    more money, less work feeding animals than people.
Johnny says, *Eeeee, I never ate so many vegetables.*
The tank top hangs lower
as his belly shrinks. Maybe he can stop
taking metformin. Maybe he can get off
the lurasidone. Maybe when he gets paid
he'll take his nephew crawdad
fishing on the ditch. Maybe someday
buy himself a little scooter
                    you know, just to get around.
Maybe one Saturday at the market
he'll find him a nice lady.

At sunrise the farmers pull up
in the boss's pickup, diesel gurgling.
Horn honks for Johnny to take his place
in back with the tiller, the boss's
sheepdog, and Freddy from Lake Street
who can't drive no more 'cause he drinks
too much in his car. No answer. Shed
door locked. Sign facedown
in the dirt. Cell goes straight
to voicemail.

On the third day Johnny
steps outside, tank top ripped, stubble,
cold sweat, scabs in his brow picked
and pulpy, stink
                    stale beer, fried weenies, burnt metal, and shame.
The demons came.

This is not Milagro. Our Johnny did not inherit
a field of beans. In this plot
            setting: South Valley, 'Burque, USA
the hero lives off the land
            in a trailer park
            a halfway house
            a shed.

His grandpa kept a small plot, enough to grow
corn, beans, squash.
            The three sisters don't mind sharing a room.

Johnny's dad wanted better
for his kids, yanked the shovel
from young Johnny's hands, said, *Go
to school, get a job with the City.
Like your cousin.*

Some on the margins never leave. They pitch a shed on a triangle of dirt
and the boundaries shift. Put their knees to the earth, the whole world
in a squash blossom, look up to find the two sisters ran off
with gabachos, sold out to developers; Daddy's land
is an apartment complex.

This state hit one hundred years. We still
don't speak American. No value,
but in things.

Johnny says, *When I sell the house, I'm gonna buy
me a trailer. I'm gonna buy me some land. Maybe
out there in the mountains.*

One year later, the sign still leans against the shed, the price
dropped from seven thousand to five. Johnny smokes
on the stoop. Guess he figured out a way to stay. Guess
the county forgot him. These things never go
according to plan.

Tan Lejos de Dios

1848 to 1912, Washington sent governors, white
elephants to mind the new territory.

English and Spanish in our Constitution. What of
Keres? Navajo? Tiwa? Tewa?

We were pueblos. We were Mexico. *Tan lejos de Dios.*
Tan cerca de los Estados Unidos.

It wasn't perfect, but we shifted
too soon—Spanish to English, communal to cash.

Parciante shovels to conservancy trucks.
Water and ejido shares for sale.

Partido, rent your sheep from the dealer,
buy your goods at the company store.

They straightened the waters,
twisted the men.

What I Know

What I know of power, I learned from Aztec goddesses
Coatlicue, snakes for skirt, morning star
claw feet, eyes in toes
feathered and furred, belt fastened with skulls
necklace of heads and hands
downward breasts and lonjas.
Serpents spring from her neck and wrists
Aztec sign of severing.
In El Museo de Antropología, she leans forward
arms poised to pounce.
Spaniards found her buried, brought her to light, buried her
again, brought up the sun stone instead, left her for Mexican
workers to dig up two centuries later.

What I know of power, I learned from Chicomecoatl
seven serpents, female spirit of corn and sustenance.
Body and face painted red, amacalli paper house headdress.
Every year I grow corn, fight
ant and grasshopper for every kernel.

What I know of power, I learned from Cihuateteo
mothers who die in childbirth, take the sun from dead warriors
beneath the earth and push it across sky.
Five days of the year
  1 Deer
  1 Rain
  1 Monkey
  1 House
  1 Eagle
they haunt crossroads
with skull face, exposed teeth, and talons
snatch children and wayward men.

What I know of power, I learned from Coyolxāuhqui
bells her cheeks, goddess of moon and Milky Way
skull at her back, snake belt at waist, breasts hang down—
Mother.

What I know of power, I learned from Tlzaoltéotl
goddess of vice, purification, steam baths, lust, midwives, filth
and patroness of adulterers
known by three names
      She Who Eats Sin
      The Death Caused by Lust
      Deity of Cotton

What I know of power, I learned from La Llorona.
She makes due in drylands, haunting alleyways and railroad tracks.

I learned from Abuela
fingerprint in empanadita edges
piecrust rolled out on formica.
She sliced through calluses with a razor blade,
slapped me once for backtalk.
Index and middle fingers tobacco-stained.
She worked the polls every election—
how I learned to vote.
The caldo she made on cloudy days is how I first loved
Brussels Sprouts, repollitos in broth.
She never attended high school.
As a girl she was hungry.
As grandmother she stocked cabinets and storage freezer—we ate
dried apricots from her kitchen months and months after she died.

I learned from Mother.

She had four boys and me, worked as a teacher's aide,
drove an hour each way to college twice a week.
She handwrote her papers in schoolgirl cursive.
She told me to stand up straight,
Be proud of your height.

I learned from my high-school self
girl in the trumpet section, bossy, talks too much in class.
I learned from Adelina Otero-Warren, Aurora Lucero, Dolores Huerta.
What I know of power, I learn from Deb, Xochitl, Michelle,
from girl I am raising
How do we grow you?
Grow ourselves?
Grow our boys to walk with you?
We plant you like corn, bathe you in sunlight, plant beans to nurture
soil, squash to shade the stalks, sprinkle water in drought, whisper
You are enough
You are enough
You are more than enough.

You Run

At sunrise, Mother next to you, Father in your heart
Somah in a ribbon shirt, her compass
tattoo points home

At sunrise, you leave
the ladder down—
other girls will climb
over walls, shatter ceilings, bore
into earth and back again

You run
a marathon
not a sprint, one day
at a time

The sun rises on Laguna, Ka'waika
in the foothills of Mount Taylor
red, yellow, orange
seed pot
made of mud, story
made of light

You take a breath
hold space with a blanket
wipe our tears on sister's scarf

The sun rises, even on Congress
on thobe, moccasins, hijab, and hoops

With Mother next to you, Somah's compass
made of mud, made of light
we know where home is, we know
our place in the universe, our right
to existence

You run
We run with you
We walk together
We take a breath
At sunrise

Muerte

Gusty Winds May Exist
Zero Visibility Possible
Fire Danger—Extreme
Beware:
      Rattlesnakes
      Lightning
      Flash Floods
      Falling Rock

Last night I dreamt your ex-wife

lived in our house. Mornings she ground
almonds with the mortar and pestle
my parents gave as a wedding gift. We tended
to her, our guest. You drove her
to the co-op for nettle and colloidal silver. I folded
her laundry, chemises in delicate squares.
She rearranged our living room, had you wrap
our microwave in foil and put it out
for trash pickup.

Before I met her, I dreamt she'd find me
in her house, sitting across the table you two shared. She
was always barefoot, hair loose, skirt
flowing, firm in showing me the door. I wanted
to know her without her knowing, see
who you were through your first love, the mother
of your children, the one who spoke
your heart into being, turned you to dust, then
spit and reshaped you again
and again until you tired of the sweeping.

Now her hair clogged the children's
bathroom sink. Afternoons
she rested on our bed, her mother visiting,
their heads touching. They shared
a cigarette and talked of the children, how tall
the boy, how beautiful the girl. Our
cat preened between them.

I took to wearing
la mano poderosa to keep
her from knowing
my thoughts. Days turned
to weeks, months.
We fell into a routine, you
cooking, me cleaning,
your ex-wife clearing our negative
entities at no charge.

One morning she packed her things in a banker's box, with a note
a man would come by to retrieve it. She
didn't know when. I drove her to the river. She handed
me her wedding band. She walked across
a sandbar. A raft of wood ducks scattered
in her wake.

Tombstone

Humans do not always live
in easily explained communities,
typecast as warriors (or princesses),
those frequently nameless, countless
brides and grooms

This is especially true here

Time erases all manufactured things
steam locomotive   kite and giant ball of string   best-of-show ribbon   jar
classes of landowners, merchants, and politicians
Christ's crown of thorns

This is especially true here

Please do not touch
bear witness   bison falling over the edge of a cliff
between figuration and abstraction
                                                  approaching storm
humanity's progression through the American West

Look for it—it is not there
plants along the road leading to Grandfather's house
some form of witchcraft,
a healing force, howling
for species and future

This is especially true here

Laborers, poor subsistence farmers saw
the crosses so often
and often in unexpected places
opulent chaos
their station in life

Mesteño

—after Luís Jimenez

Helicopter blades drown the *swish-swish* of barrenderos sweeping
night from Oaxaca streets. Eyes watered. Silly me—
it wasn't the duffel half-packed next to the bed,
the *tick-tock-tick* of my travel clock. I was leaving
the place that told me I'm beautiful, leaving
a lover—nineteen years older, a gift. He was a marine biologist,
my own Jacques Cousteau.

Our phones buzzed and beeped. Instead of copal, tear gas.
Instead of atole woman, police. Before dawn
in riot gear, with rubber bullets and clubs, they'd stormed
the zócalo where striking teachers slept on ground
under tents and tarps.

> Ántes de México, I was a plain girl, following my brother's band
> to a jazz festival in the Sacramento Mountains. Luís Jimenez
> and his wife shared my table, gave me their address
> in Hondo, said stop by anytime. I didn't know
> he was a famous artist.

I walked the zócalo with Cousteau. Café doors shuttered.
Embers. Fragments: cardboard, crate, baby bottle, belt, ladder, stake, stool. Sting.
No shoeshine boys. No globeros. No acordión, ni marimba. No fruit vendors. Hasta
las gitanas perched on gazebo steps who grabbed tourists' hands to tell
their fortunes—gone.

I emailed my parents, told them not to worry. It turns out no one
was looking for me.

> Inbox, a headline—"Chicano Artist Luís Jimenez Dies."
> A section of his sculpture fell, pinned him to the floor, severed his femoral artery.

I loved my lover's color—flor de maíz—the salted caramel of his voice, the rope
of his muscles against my hands, the way he touched my face with the backs
of his fingers that first time he asked, *¿Quieres ir a casa conmigo?*

By now Luís Jimenez was famous to me too. "El Buen Pastor."
Alligators in San Jacinto Plaza. "El Vaquero." UNM "Fiesta Dancers." He made us
big. Garish. Outlandish.

I never stopped for that visit. I held back, didn't believe his generosity.
What would I have said to him?

Fui a casa con Jacques Cousteau. He said there was a woman
in Mexico City. And was that okay? Would I
still have him? *Está bien.* And, anyway
I'm leaving.

After the zócalo, the email, and Luís Jimenez dead the way
Gloria Anzaldúa was dead, back in his bedroom
watercolor set on the bottom shelf of his nightstand.

¿También pintas?
No. Son de ella.
¿Quién es ella?
La novia.
¿La novia de quién?
Mi novia.

Taxi back to my place, duffel on the seat next to me.
Empty streets.

The artist's children and apprentices completed the sculpture. Delivered
to Denver Airport, lonely on what was
prairie, El Mesteño rears up, front hooves raised against sunset.
Red neon eyes.
Untamed.

Qué bueno que no sabía.

I didn't want to fight. I took him as he was. Older. Divorced. Spoken for. Living
in his brother's spare room. I left before it got bad. How I leave
everything. Barricades. Piles of trash. Graffiti: *Tourists, Oaxaca is temporarily closed.*
Will open when there is justice.

I miss that girl sometimes.

Buses burned. A helicopter carrying the governor crashed.
He survived. How quickly a place, a life, can change. Here then not. Blank
wall then graffiti. Lover's bed to backseat of my parents' SUV. Beautiful then
and there to what I am here.

That girl
knew
how to do for herself. She borrowed.
Something
simpler about that than keeping for herself.

And for Luís Jimenez, I learned a lesson—something about being
too big, about how your own creation can kill you,
make you bleed.

Faith

We thank the herb for giving.
A scrap of oshá in the pocket protects against snakebite.
Hierba buena soothes the stomach.
Hierba manso heals a rash.

We believe in rain, hierbas, duendes,
believe an egg rubbed over the heart puede quitar el susto,
believe a mother wanders
riverbanks crying, calling
just for us.

My Mother Was Never a Housewife

—*after Andrew Fearnside's "Succulents"*

I've killed every jade plant.
Neglect is hardest to master.
In the compost, root ball shrivels, black and black.
The last jade in a pot belonging to Grandmother.

Neglect is hardest to master.
Instructions: withhold water, as with love.
The last jade in a pot belonging to Grandmother.
She of the Kent 3 100s tended rubber tree and jalapeño.

She instructed: withhold water, showed us to parcel love
until leaves droop and trunk is hard to the touch.
She of the Kent 3 100s tended rubber tree and jalapeño.
Her love was smoke, rolling pin, burnt tortillas.

Until leaves droop and trunk is hard to the touch
succulents will lean toward the sun.
Her love was smoke, rolling pin, burnt tortillas.
My mother, her eldest, was never a housewife.

Succulents will lean toward the sun.
It's likely your indoor greenery will find you when you are least prepared.
My mother, the eldest, was never a housewife.
As a child I offered my hands. She said, *you can help best by staying out of the way.*

Your indoor greenery will find you when you are least prepared.
Dirt from your yard won't do.
I offer my hands. She says, *you can help best by staying out of the way.*
Powdery Liveforever takes decades to mature and resembles a lotus flower.

Dirt from your yard won't do.
There is a black market for succulents, crush of Korean and Chinese housewives.
Powdery Liveforever takes decades to mature and resembles a lotus flower.
Lotus, Hindu symbol of fertility

There is a black market for succulents, crush of Korean and Chinese housewives.
Separated from their cliffsides, most plants don't survive the journey.
Lotus, Hindu symbol of fertility
So much of aging is about moisture or its lack.

Separated from their cliffsides, most plants don't survive the journey.
I had a teacher who collected objects: forest rocks and petrified wood.
So much of aging is about moisture or its lack.
Like chopping the hand of a beloved and keeping it to remember her.

I had a teacher who collected objects: forest rocks and petrified wood.
The current stand of Middle Río Grande cottonwoods is nearing the end.
Like chopping the hand of a beloved and keeping it to remember her.
In the desert, every living thing asks for water.

The current stand of Middle Río Grande cottonwoods is nearing the end.
I've killed every jade plant.
Desert things ask for water.
In the compost, root ball shrivels, black and black.

El Paso Uno

Oración

El Paso del norte
pueblo del sol
pueblo de fe y familia

passageway
mythical portal

hermana de Juárez
where Mesilla Valley
holds hands with Mission Valley

You tell us what it is to be brown

⁓

El Paso, tell us
what it is to be brown

Days that burst open
A story no one wanted to write

No one woke that Saturday
wanting to be a headline

No one woke wanting
to be a back-to-school vigil

No one woke not expecting to finish sophomore year, a year that had
barely begun

No one woke that Saturday mourning
No one wanted this kind of poem
No one wanted to be a number
No one wanted

El Paso, tell us what it is
to be brown
in America

⁓

In America
He wrote a manifesto
He bought a gun

In America
burning cross
now forest

In America
He drove nine hours
A manifesto and a gun
He was arrested without incident   he drove without
        incident   he drove   he was
arrested he drove
nine hours
without incident

he wrote a manifesto
he wanted to kill
what it is to be brown
in America

Where is the wall
to keep him out?

El Paso, show us
how to be
brown
in America

⁓

Fear, where do I tuck you?

>He wrote a manifesto
>He drove nine hours

Fear, where are the exits?

He drove nine hours
He wrote a manifesto
He wanted to kill

Where brown-skinned people feel safe

If a wall could hold us
I'd build a thousand

Fear, I have bags to carry, a child's hand to guide across asphalt

Where brown-skinned people feel safe
We are flower and song
I'd build a thousand
Altars to guide us home

God gave us the Jericho story
but everything is bigger now
23 bodies

How to believe in a God stronger
than walls

Jericho, I believe what fits
in my hand, in thunderbird
rushing across red clay, believe
in the mother who names her daughter América
In the mother who whispered that Saturday, *run, mi'ja, run.*
Believe in the soldier that Saturday
who scooped up babies, ran them to safety.
Believe blood made that Walmart zócalo, campo santo, templo
sagrado.

El Paso, keeper of the sun
jagged borderlands sprinkled with Río Grande
dappled and dotted cotton fields
chiltepin pepper and Comanche prickly pear
sanctified breeze
porous grief
speak flower and song
light the dead con amor eterno

Show us
through these days that, in their senselessness, life
extinguished is a dark cloak. We are wrapped in
its despair.

Let us show you

There are days that the tragedy is too
large to bear, to shoulder alone, and we gather

in the name of prayer and poem. We gather, in the ways psalms
collect words, sacred incantations of remembrance.

We gather, because together our spirit is ineffable.
Enduring vigil, votives lit and we shall not forget.

We shall not forget that love forges on,
beyond acts of terrible violence,
beyond.

Sestina Azteca

I don't know if I buy that story
about the Aztecs mistaking Cortés for the plumed
serpent Quetzalcoatl. What with the stain
of Conquest ground
into his beard, how he couldn't speak
Nahuatl. He was the first Spanish-blood coyote

in the New World—not the canine coyotl
but trickster, story–
spinner, speaking
through Malinche, plumed
tongue from her lips to Moctezuma's ears, ground
corn passed around their circle, an offering. Scribes, their fingers stained

red and black captured this history on amate bark, stains
like coffee woven through its fibers, texture of coyote
pelt. Scribes sat on the ground,
Moctezuma on his throne, telling the story
of his people. *We come from the center of the earth. We plume*
the dead, who turn to hummingbirds. I am tlatoani,

he who speaks
for his people. They were beautiful. Market prostitute with red-stained
teeth, acupuncturist with turkey feathers
and fish spines, warriors coyote
slender and swift. We know this story,
what happens to Tenochtitlán, how it all sinks into the ground.

Today her descendants grind
teeth and bone, speak
incomplete stories.
We think we know Mexico—policía y políticos with stained
hands. Migrants pressed atop La Bestia, coyote
prey. Only feathered

beasts fly the border. The rest snatched from their children by a president's plume.
The ancestors said, yell into the ground.
Give it to Tlazoltéotl. Like coyote
she walks on all fours. She speaks
once a year, eats humanity's filth, our stains.
That's a story

I can believe. Not a plumed serpent made man who spoke
siege, who walked sacred ground and saw only the stain
of sin. But coyote woman who eats the worst of us and spits a new story.

Water

This is New Mexico. Here
life walks in circles. In drought, we
the people look to the skies,
put a hand to the ground.
In drought, we
the people
are water.

Notes

Versions of "The Color Brown," "Water," "Rain," "Tierra," "Water," "Time," "Language," "Dwelling," "*Tan Lejos de Dios*," "Muerte," "Faith," and "Water" were written as the single poem "Encantada" and presented at the Environmental Grantmakers Conference, Albuquerque, New Mexico, on September 29, 2014.

A version of "Aquí Estamos" was written and presented for Hispanic Heritage Month, Albuquerque, New Mexico, on September 6, 2018.

"A Prayer of Thanks for the Givers" was written and presented for the Maravilla Gala at the National Hispanic Cultural Center on September 4, 2018.

Versions of "Pillar of Seed," "Tierra Encantada," and "Seed Packet for Dry Land" were written for Third Thursday at the Albuquerque Museum in response to the *Climate Change: Resilience* exhibition, curated by Seed Broadcast, and performed with students in the Voces Writing Program, a project of the National Hispanic Cultural Center, on August 15, 2019.

"Bosque Walk, Groundhog Day" was written during *Walking with Poets*, cohosted by Janet Ruth on February 2, 2019.

"In Praise of Pods" was written for the Bosque Chile Festival at the National Hispanic Cultural Center and presented at the "Pods vs. Powder" Poetry Reading on August 17, 2019.

"Because the Kitchen" was written and presented for the opening of Three Sisters Kitchen, a nonprofit community food space, on August 24, 2018.

"How to Write About Service" was written for the Mayor's Day of Service on August 12, 2018; "God, has no / hands but ours, no feet / but mine and yours . . ." is adapted from a quote by Saint Teresa of Ávila.

A version of "Women's Work" was written and presented for *El Prado on the Plaza*, a traveling installation of works from Spain's Museo del Prado, on August 21, 2018.

[What is the cure for sand] was written for the *Pop-Up Poetry* installation at city-owned spaces in downtown Albuquerque and appeared on the corner Gold & 5th Street.

"Poetry Walk" was written during *Walking with Poets*, cohosted by Mari Simbaña on September 14, 2019, in response to the writing prompt "What is the name your natural surroundings call you?"

"To Grow a Child in New Mexico" was written for the 7th Annual Kids Count Conference, June 26, 2019.

"Ode to the Explorers" was written to celebrate recipients of the Jim & Mary Lois Hulsman Undergraduate Library Research Awards, University of New Mexico, April 16, 2019.

"Ode to the Art-Makers" was written to celebrate recipients of the Creative Bravos Awards, November 16, 2018.

"Ode to the Makers" was written to celebrate recipients of the Creative Bravos Awards, November 1, 2019.

"Where the Border Isn't a Metaphor" was performed at Poetry Out Loud/Lobo Slam reading, February 19, 2020.

"You Make the Library Friend" was written for the Friends of the Public Library in celebration of their fiftieth anniversary on April 27, 2019.

"Breaking Ground" was written and presented at the groundbreaking of the International District Library on May 21, 2020

"Little House 4 Sale" was presented at the Albuquerque Poet Laureate Program Pachanga de Poesía on June 16, 2020

"What I Know" was written for EKCO Poets 2020, celebrating one hundred years of women's suffrage in New Mexico and presented as part of Her Flag, created by artist Marilyn Artus and celebrating women's suffrage in the US on April 6, 2020.

"You Run" was written and presented for the district swearing-in of Congresswoman Deb Haaland, one of the two first Native American women elected to the US Congress, February 23, 2019.

A version of "Last night I dreamt your ex-wife" was written and presented for "What Is It Then Between Us?: Poetry & Democracy," organized by The Poetry Coalition, March 22, 2019.

A version of "Tombstone" was written and presented as part of the Albuquerque Museum's Third Thursday series in response to the *COMMON GROUND* and *Everyday People* exhibits, April 18, 2019. The text of the poem consists solely of phrases from exhibit labels.

A version of "Mesteño" was written and presented as part of the Albuquerque Museum's Third Thursday series, in response to works in the permanent collection, on April 18, 2019.

A version of "My Mother Was Never a Housewife" was written and presented for the Tortuga Gallery Ekphrastic Reading on August 3, 2018; italicized lines are from "How to Care for Succulents (And Not Kill Them): 9 Plant-Care Tips," www.architecturaldigest.com, and from "Species in Peril Along the Río Grande" exhibition catalog, 516 ARTS.

"El Paso Uno" was cowritten and presented with Hakim Bellamy and Jessica Helen Lopez for "22 Poems: A Reading and Vigil" to honor victims of the August 3, 2019 El Paso shooting, August 29, 2019.

"Sestina Azteca" was presented at the New Mexico State Poetry Society Annual Poets' Picnic on May 20, 2019.

Acknowledgments

The author is grateful to the editors of the following publications in which versions of these poems first appeared:

AgriCulture Journal: "Pillar of Seed"
El Palacio: "The Color Brown," "Water," "Rain," "Tierra," "Water," "Time," "Language," "Dwelling," "Tan Lejos de Dios," "Muerte," "Faith," and "Water," under the title "Encantada"
22 Poems and a Prayer for El Paso, Dos Gatos Press (2020): "El Paso Uno," cowritten with Hakim Bellamy and Jessica Helen Lopez
Malpaís Review: "Little House 4 Sale"

Agradecimientos

Los Albañiles: Dr. Shelle Sanchez and the City of Albuquerque Cultural Services Department

Los Equipos: Elise McHugh, Alexandra Hoff, and the University of New Mexico Press; The Albuquerque Poet Laureate Organizing Committee; and Jennifer Lucero

Mis Colegas: Hakim Bellamy, Jessica Helen Lopez, Manuel González, Mary Oishi

'Burque Madrinas y Padrinos: Demetria Martinez, Valerie Martínez, Mary Oishi, Margaret Randall, Levi Romero

Las Parteras: Andréa Serrano, Anel Flores, Kata Sandoval, Antionette Tellez-Humble

Chispa: Mark Rudd, your passion for the current stand of Middle Río Grande cottonwoods inspired my Poet Laureate project.

El Pueblo: TIASO, EKCO, Las Meganenas, Las Creativas, Women Writers' Collective, The U, Los Desnudos, and the Macondo Writers Workshop

Luz: The Smith's on Isleta for stocking Our Lady of Guadalupe and Sacred Heart devotional candles.

Antepasados: China y Florentino Moran and Rosaura y Pantaleón Otero

Hermanos: Frank, Tim, Mike, Daniel, I love you.

Mi Familia: In-laws, nephews, nieces, tíos, tías, and primos, thank you for attending readings, liking my social media posts, signing up for newsletters and event notifications, and reading books.

Raíces: Mom and Dad, thank you for always believing in me.

Semillas: Paloma and Kiki, my greatest teachers, you've made me a better human.

And for Henry, New Year's Eve we cast our wishes. Here is the book you wished me. Te amo.